THE HEART AND BLOOD IN YOUR BODY

RYAN NAGELHOUT

Britannica
Educational Publishing

IN ASSOCIATION WITH

ROSEN
EDUCATIONAL SERVICES

Published in 2015 by Britannica Educational Publishing (a trademark of Encyclopædia Britannica, Inc.) in association with The Rosen Publishing Group, Inc.
29 East 21st Street, New York, NY 10010

Distributed exclusively by Rosen Publishing.
To see additional Britannica Educational Publishing titles, go to rosenpublishing.com.

First Edition

Britannica Educational Publishing
J.E. Luebering: Director, Core Reference Group
Mary Rose McCudden: Editor, Britannica Student Encyclopedia

Rosen Publishing
Hope Lourie Killcoyne: Executive Editor
Kathy Kuhtz Campbell: Senior Editor
Nelson Sá: Art Director
Michael Moy: Designer
Cindy Reiman: Photography Manager

Library of Congress Cataloging-in-Publication Data

Nagelhout, Ryan, author.
The heart and blood in your body/Ryan Nagelhout. — First edition.
     pages cm. — (Let's find out! The human body)
Audience: Grades 3 to 6.
Includes bibliographical references and index.
ISBN 978-1-62275-640-7 (library bound) — ISBN 978-1-62275-641-4 (pbk.) —
ISBN 978-1-62275-642-1 (6-pack)
1. Cardiovascular system — Juvenile literature. 2. Blood — Juvenile literature. 3. Human body — Juvenile literature. 4. Human physiology — Juvenile literature. [1. Circulatory system.] I. Title.
QP103.N34 2015
612.1 — dc23
                                                                              2014021405

Manufactured in the United States of America

Photo Credits: Cover © iStockphoto.com/Eraxion; p. 1, interior pages background Cliparea Custom media/Shutterstock.com; pp. 4 Science Photo Library/Pixologicstudio/Brand X Pictures/Getty Images; pp. 5, 7 Dorling Kindersley/Getty Images; p. 6 Science Photo Library/Sciepro/Brand X Pictures/Getty Images; pp. 8, 9, 10, 12, 15, 17, 28 Encyclopædia Britannica, Inc.; p. 11 Science Photo Library/Punchstock; p. 13 BSIP/Universal Images Group/Getty Images; p. 14 Science Photo Library/Steve Gschmeissner/Getty Images; p. 16 Biology Media/Photo Researchers/Getty Images; p. 18 Ed Reschke/Photolibrary/Getty Images; p. 19 David Mack/Science Photo Library/Getty Images; p. 20 National Cancer Institute/Science Photo Library/Getty Images; p. 21 David Long/E+/Getty Images; p. 22 Tek Image/Science Photo Library/Getty Images; p. 23 Pixologicstudio/Science Photo Library/Getty Images; p. 24 Hank Morgan/Photo Researchers/Getty Images; p. 25 Darrin Klimek/Digital Vision/Thinkstock; p. 26 Spencer Grant/Photo Researchers/Getty Images.

CONTENTS

Introducing The Heart

If you sit still and put a hand on your chest, you can feel something thumping. You can even hear it if you listen carefully. The **organ** inside your chest making that noise is your heart.

The human heart is one of the most

The heart is always working to keep the body alive.

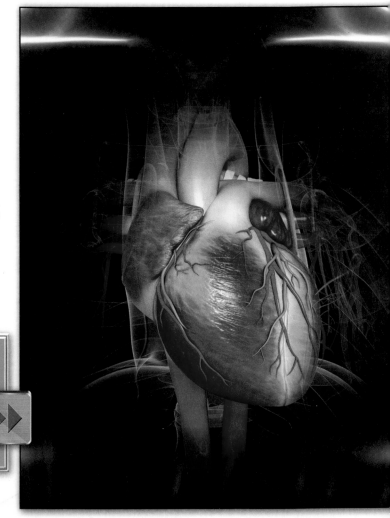

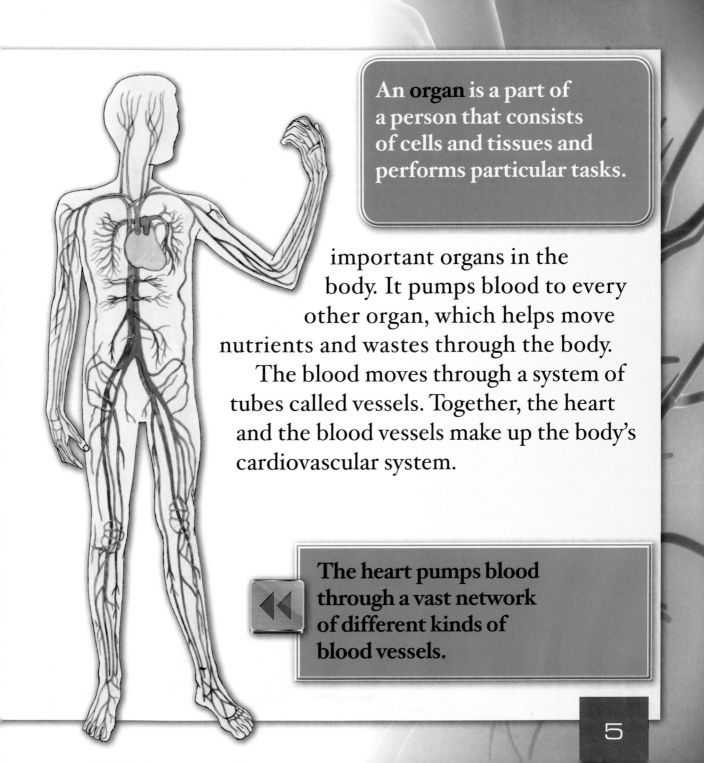

important organs in the body. It pumps blood to every other organ, which helps move nutrients and wastes through the body. The blood moves through a system of tubes called vessels. Together, the heart and the blood vessels make up the body's cardiovascular system.

The heart pumps blood through a vast network of different kinds of blood vessels.

THE HUMAN HEART

The heart is a muscle about the size of a person's fist. It is pear shaped and sits high in the chest, slightly to the left. As humans grow larger, the heart grows along with the body. The heart is made of very strong muscle. This muscle pumps blood by squeezing and relaxing in a regular rhythm. This rhythm is called the heartbeat.

A heart of an adult weighs about 8 to 12 ounces (230 to 340 grams).

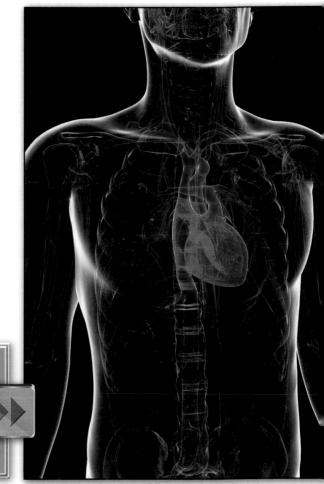

THINK ABOUT IT

The heart in a normal body at rest beats anywhere from 60 to 100 times per minute. What makes a heart beat faster?

Blood is the life fluid of the human body and the liquid that transports nutrients and removes waste. Blood travels from the heart to the lungs. In the lungs, blood releases carbon dioxide and takes in oxygen. The blood returns to the heart, where it is pumped throughout the body.

More than 4 quarts (3.8 liters) of blood pass through the heart every minute.

7

DIVIDING IT UP

The human heart is divided into right and left halves. Each half is divided into two hollow sections called chambers. The upper chambers are called atria (plural for atrium). The lower chambers are called ventricles.

Blood from the body flows into the right atrium. The blood then passes into the right ventricle, which pumps the blood to the lungs. In the lungs, blood picks up oxygen and releases **carbon dioxide**.

The heart muscle's fibers form a structure like a net. These fibers form the chambers of the heart.

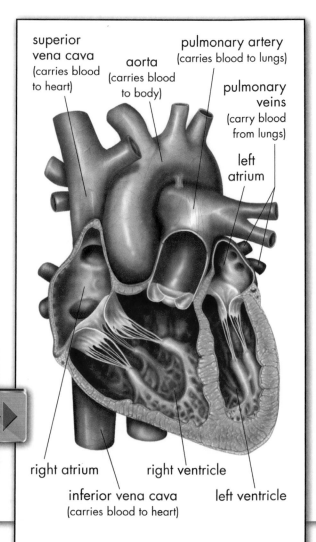

superior vena cava (carries blood to heart)

aorta (carries blood to body)

pulmonary artery (carries blood to lungs)

pulmonary veins (carry blood from lungs)

left atrium

right atrium

right ventricle

inferior vena cava (carries blood to heart)

left ventricle

Carbon dioxide is a gas that human cells make as waste. It is sent to the lungs and removed from the body when a person breathes out.

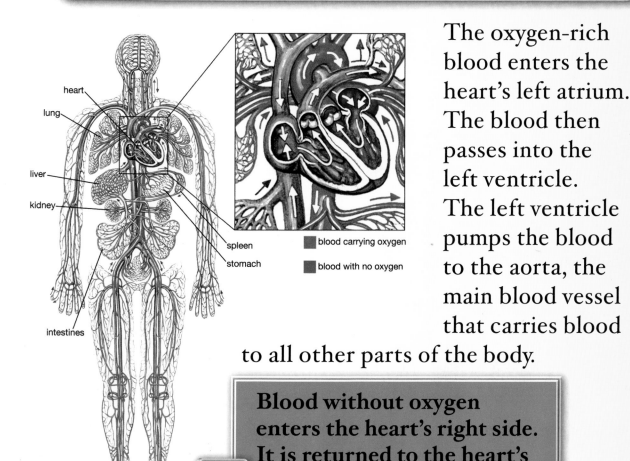

heart
lung
liver
kidney
spleen
stomach
intestines

blood carrying oxygen
blood with no oxygen

The oxygen-rich blood enters the heart's left atrium. The blood then passes into the left ventricle. The left ventricle pumps the blood to the aorta, the main blood vessel that carries blood to all other parts of the body.

Blood without oxygen enters the heart's right side. It is returned to the heart's left side after taking up oxygen in the lungs.

DOING SOME CARDIO

The heart is the main organ in the cardiovascular system. A network of blood vessels makes up the rest of the system. Blood vessels are hollow tubes that carry blood throughout the body. Blood vessels are different sizes and

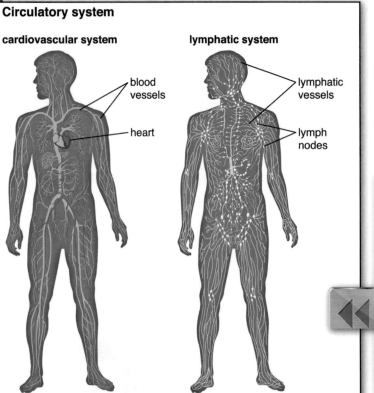

Circulatory system

cardiovascular system

blood vessels

heart

lymphatic system

lymphatic vessels

lymph nodes

The lymphatic system is part of the circulatory system. Besides lymphatic vessels, it consists of small, bean-shaped organs called lymph nodes that are found in groups throughout the body.

The **circulatory system** includes the cardiovascular system and lymphatic system. The lymphatic system, a key part of the immune system, helps the body fight diseases.

wind through the body like rivers and streams. These vessels constantly move blood in the body.

The cardiovascular system is also part of the circulatory system. The other part of the circulatory system is called the lymphatic system. The lymphatic system carries a fluid called lymph around the body. Lymph helps fight infections and is carried by lymphatic vessels. Small organs called lymph nodes are grouped in certain points along the lymphatic vessels.

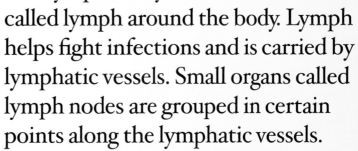

A very powerful microscope captured this image of small blood vessels moving blood in a lung.

ARTERIES, CAPILLARIES, AND VEINS

The main vessels are arteries, veins, and capillaries. Arteries carry blood out from the heart. Veins return blood to the heart. Arteries are the thickest of all blood vessels. They expand and contract to keep blood moving away from the heart. Veins contain valves that prevent blood from

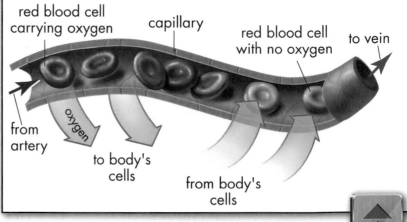

red blood cell carrying oxygen

capillary

red blood cell with no oxygen

to vein

from artery

oxygen

to body's cells

from body's cells

As blood travels through capillaries, it delivers oxygen and nutrients to the body's cells. It also picks up waste.

flowing backward. Capillaries are tiny passages that connect the arteries and the veins to the body's tissues.

In the capillaries, the blood from the arteries transfers oxygen and nutrients to cells in the tissues. The blood in other capillaries collects waste products from the cells. That blood flows into veins and back to the heart.

Veins have valves, which are flaps that can open and shut.

Blood Work

Blood makes up about 8 percent of a human's total body weight. It has many elements in it that help the body perform basic functions.

Blood carries nutrients to cells throughout the body. These nutrients come from food the person eats. The nutrients are fuel for cells to do work. Cells make waste products and blood carries them away. Waste is taken to the kidneys. The kidneys are organs that filter the blood and help remove waste from the body. Cells also produce

Blood also carries heat created by muscles and other layers of cells in the circulatory system.

THINK ABOUT IT

Which foods do you think provide your body with the best nutrients: cookies and soda or an apple and milk?

carbon dioxide. Blood carries the carbon dioxide to the lungs, which send it out of the body through breathing.

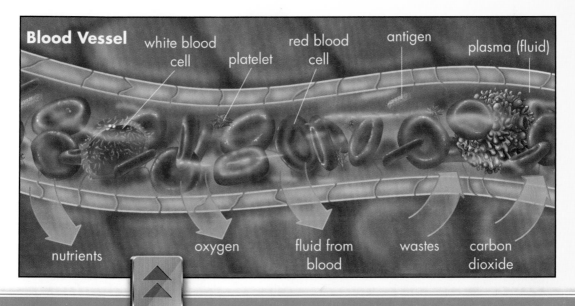

Blood Vessel — white blood cell — platelet — red blood cell — antigen — plasma (fluid)

nutrients — oxygen — fluid from blood — wastes — carbon dioxide

The walls of blood vessels are made up of living cells through which oxygen, nutrients, and waste products can pass into and out of the blood.

Blood Cells

Blood cells make up about 45 percent of the total volume of blood. Most blood cells are made inside bones in a soft, spongy tissue called bone marrow. There are three main kinds of blood cells: red blood cells, white blood cells, and platelets. Red blood cells are the most common. They are round discs with flat centers that look like shallow bowls. One drop of blood contains millions of red blood cells.

Red blood cells move oxygen through the body. In each cell,

A material called bone marrow fills the central part of certain bones. The dark red marrow is where some blood cells are made.

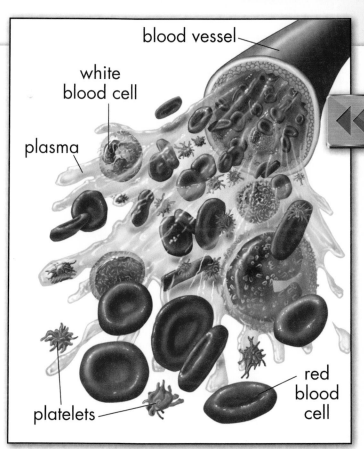

blood vessel

white blood cell

plasma

platelets

red blood cell

Blood is red because there are more red blood cells than white blood cells or platelets.

an iron-rich substance called hemoglobin carries the oxygen. Hemoglobin and oxygen together give blood its red color. Red blood cells last about 120 days before wearing out and dying. Old cells are broken down in the spleen and liver.

Think About It
Oxygen and hemoglobin combine to give blood its red color. Why is the element iron so important to a person's blood?

Blood has far fewer white blood cells than it does red blood cells. Healthy people have about 1 white blood cell for every 700 red blood cells. White blood cells help the body stay healthy. They are part of the immune system, which protects the body from foreign substances called antigens. Antigens can be any foreign material, including harmful germs, certain foods, and bee stings, that cause illness or disease.

When antigens get inside the body, white blood cells fight against them in several ways. Some swallow up the antigens. Others release proteins that attack

White blood cells are larger than red blood cells, but there are fewer of them in blood.

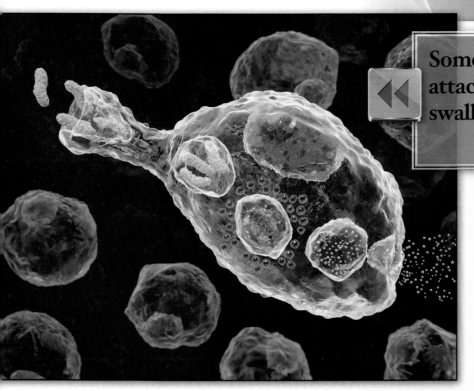

Some white blood cells attack antigens by swallowing them up.

the antigens. Some white blood cells give off substances that help the immune system attack the antigens.

Other white blood cells help break down and remove dead cells. White blood cells live for less than twenty-four hours in the bloodstream.

COMPARE AND CONTRAST
Red and white blood cells do different tasks. Other than color, how are white blood cells unlike red blood cells?

Platelets

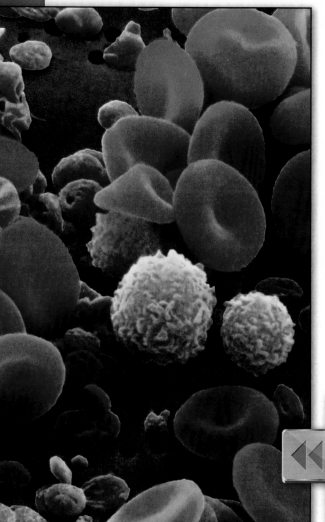

Platelets are the smallest type of blood cell. Platelets are more common in blood than white blood cells are, but they are much smaller. Platelets stick to one another and help form blood clots. Clots plug holes in the walls of blood vessels. This clotting helps stop bleeding. Platelets try to keep blood from leaving the vessels. When injured tissue triggers the clotting process,

Platelets, the small pink cells, bind together and help plug wounds in the walls of blood vessels.

THINK ABOUT IT

A bruise happens when blood vessels break and leak blood out under the skin. Why do bruises change color?

the tissue is repaired and the clot fades away. Small holes can clot naturally, but large wounds need more than just platelets to stop bleeding.

The body can make more or fewer platelets when needed.

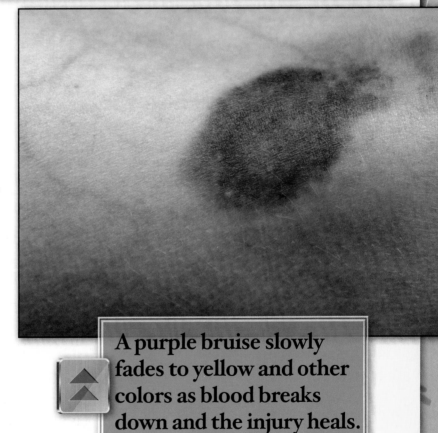

A purple bruise slowly fades to yellow and other colors as blood breaks down and the injury heals.

PLASMA

Plasma is the liquid part of blood. It carries the blood cells that move around in the blood. About 92 percent of plasma is water.

Plasma also has other material that help keep the body healthy and fuel cells. Plasma contains many different proteins. It also has nutrients such as fats,

Healthy people can donate plasma. These donations help sick people.

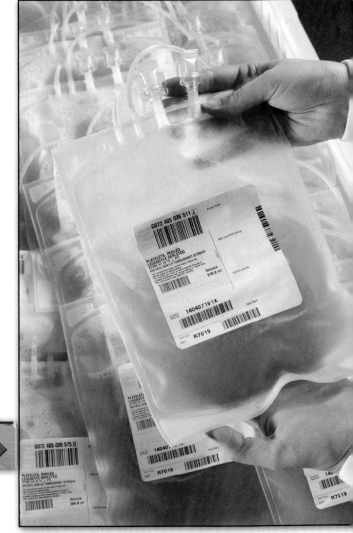

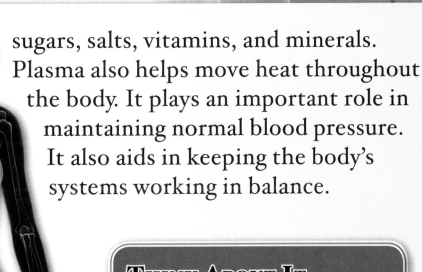

sugars, salts, vitamins, and minerals. Plasma also helps move heat throughout the body. It plays an important role in maintaining normal blood pressure. It also aids in keeping the body's systems working in balance.

THINK ABOUT IT

Plasma helps move heat throughout the body. Why do you think this task is easy for plasma to do?

Another important job plasma has is to move wastes to the kidneys, liver, and lungs, where the body can get rid of them.

BLOOD PRESSURE

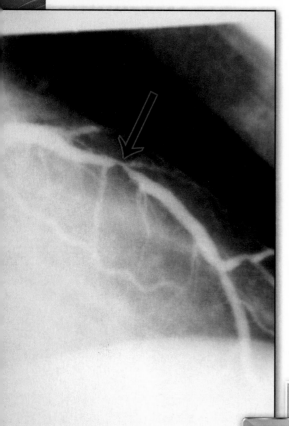

Plasma affects the body's blood pressure, which is measured by listening to the flow of blood through an artery. The body controls blood pressure through changes in heartbeat and flow of blood through the heart. When these factors change, blood pressure can be too high or too low.

High blood pressure, or hypertension, can be caused by problems with the flow of blood

A buildup of cholesterol and fats in the arteries can cause them to become narrower, which can result in high blood pressure.

Doctors fix blockages in blood vessels by transplanting, or moving, veins to make new pathways for the blood to flow through. This operation is called **bypass** surgery.

through vessels. When the force of the blood against the walls of the blood vessels is too high, a person has high blood pressure. Cholesterol, a waxy substance in blood plasma, can collect on the inner walls of arteries. Fats and other substances can collect there as well. The deposits can limit blood flow. In severe cases, this can lead to a heart attack because blood cannot flow to the heart.

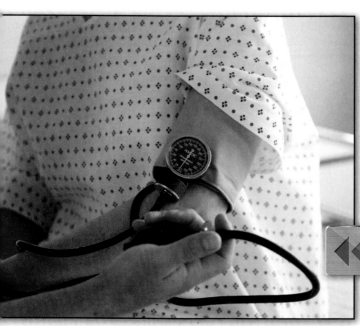

A **bypass** operation may be used to help prevent heart attacks in people who have large deposits of cholesterol or fat.

Doctors measure blood pressure using a special instrument that allows them to listen to the rushing sounds of blood.

Blood Types and Donors

The body is always making blood. As a result, some blood can be removed from the body and the body will remain healthy. People can donate blood to help others who are sick or injured. Getting someone else's blood is called a transfusion. People can also donate blood platelets and plasma.

There are four common blood groups, or types: O, A, B, and AB. Each group also has a factor that makes it positive or negative.

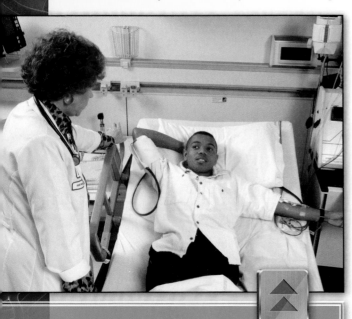

A patient receives a blood transfusion as a treatment for his blood condition.

A person with one blood type usually cannot receive blood from someone with a different blood type. This is because substances called antibodies will attack any cell in the blood that is not usually found in the body. So, a person with type B blood will have anti-A antibodies. That person cannot receive blood from a type A donor. The blood type O can be donated to people with any blood type.

THINK ABOUT IT
Type O blood can be given to people with any blood type. What type of blood can a type O person receive from a blood donor?

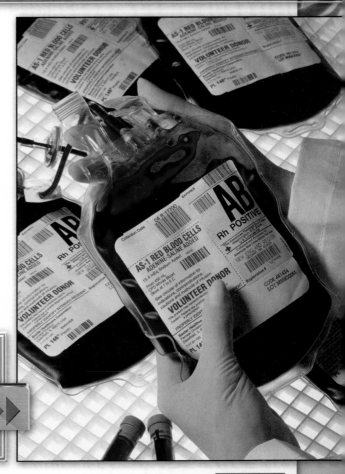

People with type AB blood can receive types AB, A, B, or O blood.

WORKING TOGETHER

The heart, blood vessels, and blood make up the cardiovascular system, which aids many other systems. Blood, the main fluid in humans, helps the lungs in

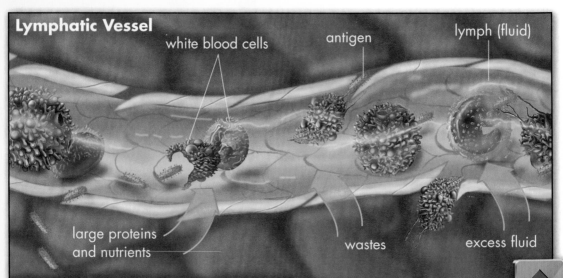

Lymphatic Vessel

white blood cells

antigen

lymph (fluid)

large proteins and nutrients

wastes

excess fluid

Lymphatic vessels and blood vessels both carry white blood cells. But lymph vessels carry lymph, not blood.

COMPARE AND CONTRAST

The cardiovascular and lymphatic systems both circulate fluids throughout the body. What is the chief difference between the two systems?

breathing and the body in removing wastes through the kidneys, spleen, and liver.

The lymphatic system is the other system that makes up the circulatory system. That system carries lymph, a pale fluid that bathes tissues. Lymph is made of white blood cells and a liquid that is like plasma. The lymphatic system helps fight infections in the body. Each system works together to keep the body alive and in balance.

Humans could not live without a healthy heart. Taking care of it and keeping the blood healthy is important to staying in shape and living a long life.

GLOSSARY

antibodies Substances made by special cells of the body that combine with an antigen and fight its effects.

aorta The main artery that carries blood away from the heart to the rest of the body.

arteries Blood vessels that move blood away from the heart.

blood vessels Small tubes that carry blood around the body.

bone marrow Soft matter inside bones where blood cells are made.

capillaries Tiny blood vessels that connect the small arteries and veins to the body's tissues.

chambers Enclosed spaces inside the heart.

diseases Illnesses that stop the body or mind from working correctly.

donate To make a gift of or to contribute.

muscle A body tissue that produces movement.

nutrients Substances that provide the body with what it needs to live and grow.

oxygen An element that is found on Earth and is necessary for life.

proteins Nutrients that the body needs to grow, repair tissues, and stay healthy.

pumps Draws, forces, or drives something onward, such as the heart pumping blood throughout the body.

relaxing Making something less tense, tight, or stiff.

rhythm A regular pattern of movement.

spleen An organ that filters the blood. It destroys worn-out red blood cells and produces some white blood cells.

squeezing Pressing something tightly.

tissues Layers of cells, usually of one kind, that form the basic structural materials of a plant or an animal.

For More Information

Books

Ballard, Carol. *What Is My Pulse?* Chicago, IL: Raintree, 2011.

Caster, Shannon. *Heart* (Body Works). New York, NY: Rosen Publishing, 2010.

Jordan, Apple. *My Heart and Blood*. New York, NY: Marshall Cavendish Benchmark, 2012.

Ollhoff, Jim. *The Heart*. Edina, MN: ABDO Publishing, 2012.

Oxlade, Chris. *The Circulatory System: Where Do I Get My Energy?* Chicago, IL: Capstone Raintree, 2014.

Slike, Janet. *Take a Closer Look at Your Heart*. Mankato, MN: The Child's World, 2014.

Storad, Conrad J. *Your Circulatory System*. Minneapolis, MN: Lerner Publications, 2013.

Websites

Because of the changing nature of Internet links, Rosen Publishing has developed an online list of websites related to the subject of this book. This site is updated regularly. Please use this link to access the list:

http://www.rosenlinks.com/LFO/Heart

Index